Feeling Great

A Girl's Guide to
Fitness, Friends & Fun

by Alyssa Shaffer

American Girl®

Published by American Girl Publishing, Inc.
Copyright © 2011 by American Girl, LLC

Questions or comments? Call 1-800-845-0005, visit our Web site at **americangirl.com**, or write to Customer Service, American Girl, 8400 Fairway Place, Middleton, WI 53562-0497.

Printed in China
11 12 13 14 15 16 17 18 19 LEO 10 9 8 7 6 5 4 3 2 1

All American Girl marks are trademarks of American Girl, LLC.

Editorial Development: Carrie Anton

Art Direction and Design: Lisa Wilber

Production: Jeannette Bailey, Judith Lary, Tami Kepler, Sarah Boecher

Photography: Steven Talley
Photography Technicians: Kristin Kurt, Travis Mancl

Special thanks to: Paula Riley; Abigail O.; Reenie M.; Maya L.; Hannah F.; Molly Barker, founder, Girls on the Run; Ronda Clements, Ed.D., program director, MAT in Physical Education and Sport Pedagogy, Manhattanville College; Julie Erasmus, instructor, Kula Yoga Center, Avon, Colorado; Dr. George Graham, professor of kinesiology, Penn State University; Dr. Teri McCambridge, chair of the American Academy of Pediatrics council on sports medicine and fitness; Dr. Gwenn Schurgin O'Keefe, CEO and editor-in-chief, *Pediatrics Now;* Heidi Skolnik, M.S., sports nutritionist

PHOTO CREDITS
The following individuals and organizations have generously given permisson to reprint images used throughout this book:
Back Cover (BC)—© iStockphoto/alsomurillo (sisters hanging out); p. 1—Ocean Photography/Veer (girls running on beach); pp. 2, 42—Polka Dot/PunchStock (girl at starting line); pp. 2, 25—Radius Images/PunchStock (girl drinking by pool); pp. 3, 14—Polka Dot/PunchStock (girl on track); p. 3—© iStockphoto LeggNet (young girl gymnast); p. 5—Fotosearch 2010 (young girl jumping for joy); p. 6—Fotosearch 2010 (young girl wearing yellow swimsuit); p. 8—Fancy Photography/Veer (three girls playing jump rope); p. 9—© iStockphoto/craftvision (finish line); p. 11—Stockbyte/PunchStock (two girl racers); p. 12—Fotosearch 2010 (family hiking through dry field); p. 17—Brand X Pictures/PunchStock (girl playing hula hoop); p. 24—© iStockphoto/pixelmaniak (popcorn); p. 31—Valueline/PunchStock (girl yawning); p. 31—Fotosearch 2010 (cocoa in glass); p. 32—© iStockphoto/MichaelWilliam (carefree); p. 34—© iStockphoto/characterdesign (young tennis player); p. 36—Corbis Photography/Veer (blond spinning in pink/gray shirt); p. 37—Brand X Pictures/PunchStock (pink boots with puppy); p. 38—BlueMoon Stock/PunchStock (three girls in karate uniforms); p. 39—Fotosearch 2010 (young girls swimming underwater); p. 41—Fotosearch 2010 (two girls sailing a small boat); p. 54—Ocean Photograpy/Veer (girl in green shirt); p. 58—© iStockphoto/gbh007 (young girl running); p. 60—Blend Images/PunchStock (girls playing soccer); p. 62—©iStockphoto/JenniferPhotographyImaging (young girl with braces writing on bed); p. 63—© iStockphoto/DonNichols (jump rope on white background)

This book is not intended to replace the advice of or treatment by physicians. Questions or concerns about physical health should always be discussed with a doctor, dietitian, or other health-care provider.

Dear Reader,

You know how good it feels to run as fast as you can on the playground, dance like crazy with your friends, splash around in the pool, or kick a ball into a goal? With all of these activities, you're getting fit.

Exercise doesn't have to be done in a gym with fancy equipment or even with a pair of sneakers on your feet! It's all about being active, moving your body, and having fun each and every day. The payoff is feeling stronger, healthier, and more confident in everything you do.

Inside these pages are lots of fantastic ideas to help you find fun ways to be active, involve your friends, fuel up for activity, and keep you feeling your best. What are you waiting for? Don't just sit there—let's get moving!

Your friends at American Girl

Contents

Fitness Is Fun!

Treat Yourself Right

Get Moving

Go for It!

Help! Q&A

Fitness Is Fun!

Exercise isn't about winning games or losing weight: it's about moving your body and feeling great.

Fitness Facts

1. You don't have to do it all at once.

Some people think exercising means lifting weights, running miles, and swimming laps. While those are examples, what's more important is just getting your body moving. You should try to be active for about 60 minutes a day, but that doesn't mean you have to exercise all in one session. Break it up into small chunks: Run around for 15 minutes at lunchtime. Play games with your friends for at least 15 minutes after school. Walk home, to the library, or around the neighborhood with a friend for 15 minutes. After you do your homework, jump rope for 15 minutes. It all counts!

2. It will help you get more ZZZs.

Being active during the day can help you fall asleep faster and tone down nighttime tossing and turning, so that you wake up feeling energized and ready to go.

3. It will help boost your brain power.

Research shows that being physically active can help you do better on math, English, and other standardized tests, as well as get higher grades.

4. You'll feel happier.

Ever hear of a "runner's high"? Studies show that your brain actually gets a burst of feel-good chemicals when you exercise for at least 30 minutes—and you don't even have to be running.

5. You'll be healthier now and when you're older, too.

Get moving today to help your body for years to come. Regular activity builds stronger bones, protects your heart and lungs, and helps prevent or regulate diseases such as diabetes.

6. It doesn't have to be hard to be effective.

You don't have to be gasping for air or think you're about to pass out. (Actually, that means you're probably working way too hard!) All you need is to move at a brisk pace—that means if you're chatting with a friend while you're exercising, you might feel just a little out of breath. The more you get out and get moving, the easier it should get!

7. It isn't about changing your body.

Being fit doesn't mean focusing on losing weight or how you look in a swimsuit. It's about how you feel—strong, happy, healthy, and proud!

Quiz
Fit for You

1. When I think about getting ready for an activity, I usually

   a. reach for a ball or my uniform.

   b. grab my sneakers.

   c. don't change out of what I already have on.

2. If I'm hanging out with my friends, we like to

   a. split up into teams and play kickball.

   b. get on our bikes or scooters and race around the park.

   c. put on some music and dance.

3. On the weekends, you can usually find me

   a. at practice.

   b. going on a hike with my family.

   c. chilling out at home.

4. If I have to be in a competition or contest in school, I usually feel

   a. very excited! I love to practice for the big day and try to win.

   b. nervous! I usually start out with a few butterflies but relax once I get started.

   c. horrified! I hate competition and would give anything not to participate.

5. Which of the following is your favorite way to get sweaty?

   a. Practicing drills or doing whatever else my coach tells me to do

   b. Running through a backyard obstacle course I made with my friends

   c. Yuck! I hate to get sweaty!

6. When it's team time in gym class, I usually feel

   a. charged up. I love it when we play games and pick teams.

   b. so-so. I like moving around, but I don't love it when I have to compete with my friends.

   c. bummed out. I hate team sports.

Answers

Team Player

If you answered **mostly a's,** you love to play to win. Since you like the thrill of competition and know how to handle defeat, try out in school or with a community league for your favorite sport, whether it's soccer, softball, hockey, basketball, lacrosse—you name it. Experiment with a few to see what you like best, and practice with your friends or family to keep your skills up when you're not in a game. Just don't be too hard on yourself. Remember, it's more important to get out and have fun than to win each time!

Real Mover

If you answered **mostly b's,** you like to walk, jog, hike, bike, and just get going with your friends. But you're not so into structured activities—you'd rather have fun on your own than with a team. So play around! Go bowling with your BFFs, jump rope during recess, or toss a football around with a family member before dinner. If you're on your own, see how long you can twirl a hula hoop or how many times you can bump a volleyball in the air without dropping it. Then try to beat your own records. There's no limit to what you can do, and it never hurts to try something new!

Free Spirit

If you answered **mostly c's,** you don't usually have an exercise plan, and you're not into organized sports or activities. You just like to have fun dancing to music or goofing around with your friends and family. So go do it! You don't have to be involved with a team or do things like jumping jacks and sit-ups to be fit. Just find ways to move your body every day for at least 60 minutes. Try sledding with a bunch of friends, cleaning your room as fast as you can, or giving your little brother piggyback rides in the backyard. You can do your own thing and still be a fitness superstar!

What Should I Do?

Some of us crave speed, some of us love to be outside, some of us can't wait to compete, and some of us would rather just hang out and take it slow. And, depending on the day, we may want to do some or all of these! Choose what you love and find the perfect activity to match your mood. Then go ahead and give it a try—and don't limit yourself to just one thing.

Are you a thrill seeker?

Try snowboarding, skiing, kite boarding, speed skating, skateboarding, roller derby, surfing—anything that has some speed and gives you a rush. Grab safety gear and get your parents' permission to challenge yourself with something new and gravity-defying!

Are you relaxed and laid-back?

Try walking, running, yoga, golfing, sea kayaking, or tai chi. They're all great ways to relax, have fun, and focus on what you're doing.

Are you competitive to the core?

Try soccer, softball, basketball, tennis, cheerleading, gymnastics, field hockey, volleyball, swimming—activities with a coach who can help you perform at your best. Don't be afraid to try a new sport—you never know what you might be good at.

Are you a music lover?

Try dancing on your own, having a dance-a-thon or a dance-off with a friend, twirling a hula hoop to music, or choreographing your own cheerleading routine. Just put on some music and get moving!

Are you a great-outdoors girl?

Try hiking, biking, rock climbing, cross-country skiing, canoeing, horseback riding—they're all great ways to get outside and away from it all.

Are you a super friend?

Try gathering your pals for hopscotch, riding scooters, skating, running around the playground, playing badminton or croquet, or shooting hoops. The more friends, the better!

17

Go for Your Goals

When you set a goal for yourself—whether it's swimming a full lap in the pool without stopping, trying to win a trophy with your teammates, or mastering a cartwheel or handstand—it makes staying active easier and can give you an amazing sense of accomplishment. Take a few minutes to set three different activity goals for yourself using the prompts on pages 4–5 of the *Goal Guide*. Be specific and give yourself enough time to achieve each goal, but don't be afraid to challenge yourself! Here's an example:

Reach Your Goals

What do you really want to do?
Write it down now.

My **first** activity goal is to

I want to do this because

I will do this by

If I need help, I will

My second activity goal is to

I want to do this because

Girl goals:
Choose your challenge

Not quite sure what goals to go for? They don't have to be complicated or anything big! Start by choosing something you've always wanted to try or a skill you've wanted to improve. Here are some ideas:

• Jump rope 25 times without stopping. Work up to 100.

• Stand on one foot for 15 seconds, then 30, then 45, and then one minute. Then start over with your eyes closed.

• Shoot a basket from the free-throw line. If your shot isn't close, start with throwing closer to the net and moving back after each shot goes through the hoop. When you make it to the free-throw line, try making as many baskets in a row as you can—set your own record.

• Start a walking club with friends. Set team distance goals for walking together.

• Learn how to ice-skate. Then try going backward.

• Get your whole family to go for a long bike ride.

• Try one new activity you've never tried before but were always curious about—racquetball, rowing, Ultimate Frisbee—the possibilities are endless!

Girl Profile

My goal: Run a 5K (3.1-mile) race in about 30 minutes

Why I chose it: I had never really run a long-distance race before, and I thought it would be fun to try! I signed up with Girls on the Run, a group that helps girls ages 8–13 train for a 5K in 12 weeks through group workouts.

My favorite part of training: I liked hanging out with my friends. I knew some girls before I started, but then I made a lot of new friends, too. It was great having so many people around me, all with the same goal.

What I didn't like: I didn't really want to run sometimes, or it felt too hard. On those days, I paired up with a friend and talked as we moved. It made the hard training days easier and more fun.

Something I learned: It's not related to running, but I learned how to stick up for myself. Our coaches were great to talk to, and I would go to them if someone was being mean to me in school. They would help me figure out what to say.

What I'll always remember: The best part was crossing the finish line. I ran the race with my dad, and everyone was cheering me on like crazy. I finished the race in 30 minutes and 32 seconds. After the race, a bunch of my friends came up to me to congratulate me. One of my friends said that she wanted to do it with me again next year!

My next goal: I want to become a better swimmer.

Stay fit, strong, and ready to move! Here's what you need to know to keep your body at its best.

Start Smart

Don't burn out before you begin!

To get fueled up and stay energized, have some water and a light snack about an hour before you exercise. Here are some yummy treats to try:

- two pieces of fruit leather (made with real fruit)
- a cottage cheese snack cup topped with sliced bananas
- a small granola bar
- a piece of string cheese and a few whole-grain crackers
- a small snack-size bag of whole-grain cereal and pretzels mixed with raisins for a sweet-salty combo
- a cup of unbuttered popcorn sprinkled with Parmesan cheese

Don't start with a sprint

When it comes to exercise, it's best to start slowly. Try a 10-minute *warm-up,* which is when you gradually work harder to bring more blood and oxygen to your muscles. This will help your body perform at its best and keep you from getting hurt. To warm up, try walking around or jogging in place.

On the go? Drink up!

Take a few sips of water every 15 minutes or so when you're moving around—especially if it's hot or humid. And don't wait until you're thirsty. Feeling thirsty usually means you're already dehydrated, which can leave you cranky, light-headed, and nauseated. Sports drinks are a good option, because they contain salts and other minerals that help you stay hydrated. Avoid caffeinated beverages and energy drinks.

25

Solo Stretches

Stretching is the one thing people often skip in their work-outs, but it's important to keep your muscles flexible and help you perform at your best.

Stretches to get going

When your muscles are warmed up, try some *dynamic stretches*—controlled leg and arm movements.

Arm circle jog

Muscles stretched: shoulders, chest, upper back

Goal: Do two combos of forward and backward arm circles for 10–15 seconds each.

Jog in place while swinging arms in large circles.

Lift and kick

Muscles stretched: front and back of legs

Goal: Do three combos of lift and kicks for 10–15 seconds each.

Walk in place, lifting knees as high as you can. Then jog in place, kicking heels toward your butt.

LIFT — WALKING KNEE-THIG
KICK-JOGGING BUTT-KIC

Stretches to cool down

At the end of your workout is another great time to stretch. *Static stretches*—stretches that you hold in place—help bring your heart rate down and slow your breathing.

L stretch

Muscles stretched: *hamstrings* (the muscles along the backs of your thighs)

Goal: Hold 20–30 seconds per leg.

Lie on the floor with legs straight out. Raise one leg, grasping both hands behind the thigh. Keep the floor leg straight as you gently pull the raised leg toward your belly. Repeat with opposite leg.

Cross-arm stretch

Muscles stretched: upper back and shoulders

Goal: Hold 20–30 seconds per arm.

Stand with your right arm in front of your chest. Place your left forearm on your right forearm, and gently pull your right arm toward your body. Repeat with opposite arm.

27

Double flamingo

Muscles stretched: *quads* (the muscles along the fronts of your thighs)

Goal: Stretch each leg for 20–30 seconds.

Stand facing your friend, with your left hand on her left shoulder and her left hand on your left shoulder. Lift your right leg (your friend does the same), bending the knee and holding the top of your right foot or ankle. Bring your right heel to your butt, stretching the front of your leg. Help each other stay balanced while you hold the stretch.

Twist and turn

Muscles stretched: back, chest, shoulders

Goal: Stretch for about 20–30 seconds, then switch arm positions and repeat.

Sit cross-legged facing your friend, so that your knees are touching your friend's knees. Reach your right arm around your lower back as your friend does the same. Then reach your left hand and grab your friend's right hand as she grabs your right hand with her left hand. Look over your left shoulders, pulling against each other gently to feel a stretch along your backs.

Partner pull

Muscles stretched: upper back, shoulders, quads

Goal: Stretch for about 20–30 seconds, and then sit back up. Switch hand positions and repeat.

Facing your friend, kneel down, sitting back on your heels. Slide your feet out so that you're sitting on the floor between your feet. Lift your arms in front of you.

Hold your friend's right hand on top and your left hands together underneath. Both of you lean back, tucking in your chins. Pull gently on each other's hands to feel the stretch in your backs and along the fronts of your legs.

Finish Right

When you're done

During exercise your heart beats extra fast. Before you call it quits, bring your heart rate down by cooling off with a few minutes of light walking, slower movements, or more stretches.

Grab a snack

Now's the time to refuel with some good food. Nutrients like *carbohydrates* (an energy source found in foods like bananas, pasta, and pretzels) and *protein* (essential compounds found in foods like milk, meat, and beans) are important because they help rebuild your muscles and get you ready for your next activity! Try to eat something within a two-hour period after you're done exercising, such as

- a yogurt parfait made by sprinkling fresh fruit and granola into your favorite flavor of yogurt
- half an English muffin topped with peanut butter
- trail mix made with dried fruit, nuts, and chocolate chips
- rice or popcorn cakes topped with spreadable cheese
- a smoothie made with frozen fruit and milk or yogurt
- scrambled eggs and whole-wheat toast
- cereal and milk
- apple slices with peanut butter

Head to bed

Not everyone likes an early bedtime, but when you're exercising or playing sports you need more sleep than ever. Experts say to get anywhere from 8 to 12 hours a night, depending on your age and how you feel. If you've ever nodded off in homeroom, taken a quick snooze in the car on the way home, or just felt kind of worn out throughout the day, you probably need a bit more pillow time.

Science Says So: Make It Chocolate Milk

A glass of chocolate milk is a perfect post-exercise drink. Scientists say the combo of protein found in milk and carbs found in the sugars of chocolate syrup help repair and rebuild muscles.

Get Moving

Start here for some simple ways to spring into action.

20 Ways to
Be Fit & Have Fun

Sports and stuff

1. Hit a tennis ball against an outside wall. See how many times you can do it without missing.

2. Power up in 5: Do 5 push-ups, 5 jumping jacks, 5 *frog jumps* (squat down and jump forward), and 5 sit-ups. Try to do all the exercises 5 times through.

3. Get fit while you sit! Sit on an *exercise ball* (a large inflatable ball, also called a stability ball) while you do your homework or watch TV. You'll strengthen your stomach muscles as you sit tall and stay balanced! For a challenge, lift one or both feet and see how long you can keep your balance.

4. Grab a jump rope and try some tricks! Try skipping, hopping on one foot, crossing the rope, or jumping side to side like a skier. Have some friends hold the rope and try turning in a circle each time you jump, or jump while holding a partner's hands.

5. Have a mini-tournament in the pool with your friends. See who can swim across the pool the fastest, or who can do the most handstands and somersaults, and then do a dance routine together.

6. Sign up for a bike-a-thon, charity walk, or fun run with a parent, and then train together at least once a week.

7. Take the stairs! Find a set of stairs and run all the way up. Time yourself to see how long it takes.

8. Assign exercises to the different suits of a deck of cards. For example: push-ups for hearts, sit-ups for spades, jumping jacks for clubs, and leg lifts for diamonds. Shuffle the deck and then pick a card to see what exercise you should do and how many times to do it. If you pull an eight of hearts, do eight push-ups. Face cards are worth ten. See how many you can get through. After a few rounds, come up with new exercises.

Go high-tech

9. Get a pedometer, strap it on, and see how many steps you take during the day. Then see if you can add another 100 steps tomorrow. Every 2,000 steps is about one mile.

10. Challenge your mom, dad, or big sister or brother to a Wii™ sports game. Don't cheat—move your whole body, not just the remote.

11. Create a playlist of fast and slow songs. Then go for a walk or jog on a treadmill, letting the music set your pace—every time the beat speeds up, so do you!

Be silly

12. Set up an obstacle course in your backyard. Run around a tree, jump over some rocks, skip backward 10 steps, and try a cartwheel. Race a friend or time yourself, and try to set your own personal record!

13. Go with a parent on a neighborhood scavenger hunt. Try to locate the items below. Make a checklist, and take a picture or cross off each item when you find it.

   - a flower
   - a dog
   - a fire hydrant
   - a red car
   - a mailbox
   - a newspaper box
   - a slide
   - a clover patch
   - someone wearing sunglasses
   - a baby stroller

14. Have a dance-a-thon. Make up a playlist of your favorite songs (or put on a radio station that you love) and dance through at least five songs in a row.

15. Walk an imaginary tightrope. Try to walk in a straight line, heel to toe, and pretend you're on the high wire. See how long you can go without stepping out of line.

16. Play monster freeze tag. Have some fun with younger siblings or the little kids in your neighborhood. Be the monster who's It and tag anyone who's not on base to freeze them. Anyone who's not frozen can leave base to unfreeze their friends, but they risk getting tagged by you.

Help out around the house

17. Walk the dog around the block. No pooch of your own? Ask a friend who has a dog if you can join her.

18. Wash the car. Suds it up with some elbow grease, and then spray it off. Getting wet is part of the fun!

19. Rake leaves into a big pile. Before you bag them, jump on in.

20. Clear some clutter! Put on some music and time how long it takes to make your bed and put away all your stuff. Try to beat your time each time you clean.

Have More
Fun with Friends

The more you enjoy the exercise you do, the more likely you'll stick with it long-term. Since lots of things are more fun with a friend, find a pal to partner with when you work out. Try these ideas to build strong bonds with the friends you have and maybe make some new friends, too.

Take a class

When you sign up for a class, whether it's learning a new type of dance or trying a martial arts style, you'll be sure to make new friends who share some of your interests. If you're nervous about trying something new alone, ask a friend to take a class with you. An instructor can teach you both the ins and outs of whatever you decide to try. Check out your local parks and recreation centers to see what kinds of classes they offer.

When you exercise with a partner, you both win.

Join a team

When you're on a team, you never have to worry about competing by yourself. Your teammates will be there to support you and cheer you on—and you have the chance to be there for your friends, too! Plus, a coach can help you learn how to make smart decisions when you train and play. Teams come in many forms, from traditional sports like soccer, volleyball, swimming, and basketball to something out of the ordinary, like a hip-hop dance team.

Play a game

Boredom-busting games are a great way to get your group of friends moving together.

Balloon on a Spoon

Have players divide into two teams and line up. Provide a bucket of water balloons for each team. Mark a finish line about 10 yards away. The first person on each team balances a balloon on a plastic spoon and races to the finish line. If she breaks the balloon, she must go back to the start and get a new one. The first team with all players across the finish line is the winner.

Frisbee Challenge

Play a game of H-O-R-S-E with a Frisbee and an empty box. Call the shot and then challenge your friends to get the Frisbee into the box the same way. Each time one of you misses, you get a letter. The last one to spell HORSE wins!

Cat and Mouse

Choose one person to be the "mouse," while the remaining players divide into pairs of "cats." The object of the game is for one pair of cats to join hands around the runaway mouse to "catch" her. When the mouse is caught, select a new mouse and new pairs of cats.

Sign up for camp

When you go to a specialized camp, you'll make a boatload of new friends from places near and far. Together, you can do tons of activities, whether you're looking for something special or want a mix of a few different things. Below are a few fun new things you can try at camp. If any of them seem interesting to you, talk to your parents about how to get started.

- sailing
- lacrosse
- beach volleyball
- circus arts
- dance
- wakeboarding

- ice-skating
- martial arts
- cheerleading
- fencing
- skiing
- windsurfing

Go for It!

Your body is amazing, so put it to the test.

Muscle Power

Toned muscles can help you do better in sports and activities, build stronger bones, and keep you healthier. You don't have to go to the gym or lift weights; your body can provide all the resistance you need! While there are all kinds of ways to make your muscles stronger, the following are a few exercises to try two or three times a week. (If you're not sure how to do them, ask a parent to show you.)

Stand and sit

Muscles worked: quads, *glutes* (butt muscles)

Goal: 10 repetitions

a. Stand with your hands in front of you and your feet about the same distance apart as your shoulders.

b. Bend your knees and sit back, as if you were about to sit down in a big chair. Try to keep your weight over your heels, using your arms for balance. Look down at your toes—you should be able to see them past your knees. Stand back up and repeat.

Lunges

Muscles worked: glutes, thighs, *calves* (lower rear leg muscles)

Goal: 10 steps for each leg

a. Stand with your feet hip-distance apart and your hands on your hips. Take a step forward with your left foot, bending both knees. Keep your front knee over your ankle, not past your toes.

b. Straighten your legs and bring your right foot to meet your left. Then take a big step forward with your right foot. Repeat.

Pair Up

Two-in-one squat

Muscles worked: hips, glutes, and fronts of legs

a. Stand facing your partner about an arm's length apart. Keep your feet about shoulder-distance apart. Hold onto each other's forearms.

b. Bend your knees, as if you were sitting back into a chair, keeping your knees above your ankles (you should be able to see your toes if you look down). Hold 5 seconds and then stand back up. Repeat 10 times.

Aches or Pain?

It's normal to feel slightly sore or achy after exercise, but if you experience any of the following problems, tell your parents and coaches or teachers right away:

Find a friend and try these takes-two exercises.

Ball over-under

Muscles worked: back, butt, and backs of legs

a. Get a ball, such as a basketball, soccer ball, or playground ball. Stand with your feet about shoulder-distance apart, back to back with your partner. Raise your arms overhead and grab the ball from your partner.

b. Bend forward and pass the ball to your partner through your legs. Stand up and repeat for 20–30 seconds, then switch so that your partner passes first.

- any pain following a popping sound
- sharp pain going up or down stairs
- limited range of motion, such as discomfort moving your arms or wrists in a full circle
- any swelling

Yoga for You

Yoga is a great way to stretch your muscles, relax, recharge, and sometimes turn your world upside down! Find space on the floor, take off your shoes and socks, and try these four poses.

Tree pose

What it does: helps improve balance

Goal: Hold the pose on each leg for three or more breaths.

a. Stand tall with your hands on your hips. Bring the heel of one foot against the inside of your lower opposite leg.

b. Bring your palms together in front of your chest, and if you can, slide the bottom of your foot up to the inside of your opposite thigh with your bent knee pointing out to the side. (Be sure not to place your foot on the inside of your knee.) To help you stay balanced, look at a point just ahead of you on the floor. Breathe deeply in and out. Switch legs and repeat.

Dancer pose

What it does: helps you get stronger and more flexible while improving balance

Goal: Hold the pose on each leg for three or more breaths.

a. Stand tall with your hands down at your sides. Bend your right knee and grab your right foot behind you with your right hand. Take a moment to find your balance.

b. Straighten your left hand in front of you as you keep lifting your right foot behind you. Breathe deeply in and out. Switch legs and repeat.

49

Bridge pose

What it does: helps strengthen legs and glutes while stretching your back

Goal: Stay in this pose for a few breaths.

a. Lie on your back with knees bent and feet on the floor, about the same distance apart as hips. Keep arms straight on the floor.

b. Pressing your feet into the floor, lift your hips and back, leaving your arms and hands flat on the floor. When you're ready, slowly roll your spine back down to the floor.

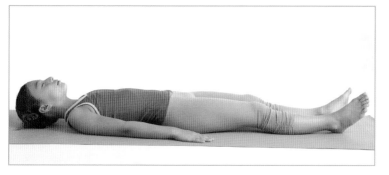

Resting pose

What it does: helps you relax and get re-energized

Goal: Stay in the pose for about 5 minutes.

a. Lie faceup on the floor with your hands at your sides. Let your feet fall naturally to either side. Try to relax your whole body while breathing deeply and evenly.

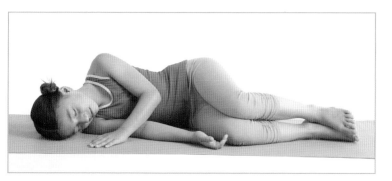

b. When you're ready, wiggle your fingers and toes, and then bring your knees to your chest and roll to one side. Slowly sit up.

Girl Profile

Why I started doing yoga: I play soccer, and my mom, who also does yoga, thought that I would really like it and that yoga might help my game. I usually take an hour-long class once a week after school with a bunch of other kids my age.

What I like about it: It feels good when I'm doing it. The poses help me stretch different parts of my body. And I feel really great when I'm done!

Favorite yoga pose: Pigeon. It's a stretching pose that puts you in kind of a weird position, but it really helps loosen you up. I also really like Crow, where you balance on your arms and lift your legs. You're building strength but in a totally different way from anything else.

What I've taken from the class: Yoga has really helped in some of the other sports I play. I feel as if I have more energy to run and score points in soccer, and I have more arm strength, which can help me make shots from farther away when I play basketball.

Hardest part: The resting pose. We do it at the beginning, and it's hard to just lie there and keep your eyes closed. But at the end it's great—you really do feel totally relaxed!

What I learned: I learned how to breathe more evenly. Sometimes when I'm running in soccer I'll get out of breath, but taking yoga helped me learn how to control my breathing so that I could run harder. It also helps if I get stressed out. I just remember to take a deep breath, and I feel a little calmer.

What I didn't like: I'm not very flexible, so some of the poses were a little hard to do. But the more I practiced, the more poses I could do.

Get anwers to questions about fitness and exercise here. Still don't see what you really want to know about? Check with a parent, doctor, coach, or other trusted grown-up. Good info is always important!

Your Body

Should I exercise when I'm not feeling well?
—Under the Weather

If you have a slight cold or just some sniffles, you're probably fine, but if you're nauseated, have a fever, or just feel really sick, your body is telling you it needs to rest. And remember, it can take some time to get well—you may feel better the next day, or it may take up to a week or more until you're back to 100%. Talk to a grown-up to sort out your symptoms and make sure you're not doing too much too soon, or you may just get sicker.

What's the best way to keep from getting hurt while doing sports? —Health Nut

Don't overdo it! Your body is changing, which can make you more open to injury. Be sure to get lots of rest in between workouts, practices, and games. Just as the pros take downtime after their seasons are done, young athletes should take 2 to 3 months off each year. In the meantime, try a different type of activity, even if it's just playing games with your friends outside. And if you do feel that something hurts, rest until it stops being painful. Otherwise a minor injury can become a major one before you know it.

A little TLC can keep you feeling healthy and strong.

I like exercising, but is there such a thing as working out too much? — Always on the Go

Absolutely! While you should try to do some activity about an hour a day, just riding your bike, dancing around with your friends, and playing outside can be enough. If you lift weights or work your muscles, try not to exercise the same way two days in a row. And if you're very busy or active one day, take it easier the next. Your body needs time to rest and recover.

Fitness Facts

I like to run but I get tired really easily. How can I run farther without getting out of breath?

—Catching My Breath

You don't start reading without knowing your ABCs, and the same thing goes for any type of exercise. Start with the basics and work your way up. Your lungs need to get used to breathing harder, and your heart needs to get used to pumping more blood to the exercising muscles. Begin by doing a fast walk around a track or with an adult around your neighborhood. Then work your way up to jogging for a minute or so before going back to a brisk walk. As it gets easier, make those jogging times longer and the walks shorter. Pretty soon you'll be able to mostly jog, which you can then turn into a faster run. *If you continue to be out of breath in your training, tell a parent.*

I'm sometimes sore after I exercise. What can I do to help? — Feeling Achy

It's no fun to feel sore, but the good news is that the aches usually mean your body is just recovering from your exercise. Your muscles actually break down and rebuild when they are challenged, which can cause some of that next-day muscle soreness, but that also means you're getting stronger. Give yourself some time to recover by doing something casual, such as going for a ride on your scooter with your friends. If you still feel achy, rest and take a warm bath. Having some protein-rich foods, such as a glass of chocolate milk, a PB&J on whole-wheat bread, a cheese stick, or some turkey slices on crackers can also help get your muscles the material they need to recover. *If the pain feels sharp or it doesn't go away after a couple of days, tell a grown-up.*

Is there a best time of the day to exercise? — Morning Girl

Yes—the time that works best for you! Seriously, it doesn't matter if you're a morning bird, a night owl, or something in between. What's important is just doing *something*, even if it's just for a few minutes at a time.

Good Sport

I've joined so many sports and activities that I've gotten way behind on my schoolwork. How can I manage to keep playing and still get good grades? —Busy Bee

Sometimes you can have too much of a good thing. While it's great that you're interested in trying out a lot of activities, it's also easy to get overwhelmed when you add in homework, friends, and family. Pick one or two sports or activities each season that you enjoy and weed out the rest. Try doing your homework as soon as you get home so that you get it out of the way. If you're already behind, talk to your teachers about extra-credit work to catch up. Be sure to put your schoolwork first or pretty soon you may find that you won't get to play at all!

Connect with your friends, manage your schoolwork, and play at your best—here's how.

My friend and I are competitive in sports.
We don't fight about it, but there's always
a lot of tension between us. What should I do?
—Out to Win

It's natural to feel competitive when you play sports, even with your friends and teammates. The goal of any team is to work together so that you can all perform at your best. Be honest and talk to your friend about your feelings— you'll both feel better after clearing the air. Remember that true friends support each other through rough spots and cheer on each other's successes, no matter what.

Even though I try my hardest, my teammates say
I have to do better. How can I improve so that I
won't disappoint my friends? —Worried

It's great that you make a big effort with each practice and game. But don't be afraid to ask for help. You don't need to hire a private coach to put you through hours of practice— sometimes even asking someone close to you for some playing tips can make a big difference. Talk to your coach to see if she can think of anything to work on. And remember that your teammates are there to give you support, not tear you down.

> *"It's a **dream** until you write it down, and then it's a **goal**."*
>
> —Anonymous

Is there something you've always wanted to do but never dared to try? It could be as simple as learning how to swim or as magical as winning a gold medal. Whatever you dream of, it all starts with a plan of action. Use the included *Goal Guide* to help you reach your goals, whether near or far, large or small.

Write to us!
Tell us how you're staying active!
Send your thoughts to
Feeling Great **Editor**
American Girl
8400 Fairway Place
Middleton, WI 53562

(All comments and suggestions received by American Girl
may be used without compensation or acknowledgment.
Sorry—photos can't be returned.)

Here are some other American Girl books you might like:

❑ I read it.

❑ I read it.

❑ I read it.

❑ I read it.